Echoes of Vietnam | A Soldier's Voice is Heard

Ronald Kays

Published by RGK Publishing, 2024.

While every precaution has been taken in the preparation of this book, the publisher assumes no responsibility for errors or omissions, or for damages resulting from the use of the information contained herein.

ECHOES OF VIETNAM | A SOLDIER'S VOICE IS HEARD

First edition. August 26, 2024.

Copyright © 2024 Ronald Kays.

ISBN: 979-8223256335

Written by Ronald Kays.

Table of Contents

To Vicki, always my Encourager in Chief. I love you.

ECHOES OF VIETNAM

A Soldier's Voice Is Heard

Ronald G. Kays with Roger B. Kays, Major, U.S. Army *(Retired)*

FOREWORD

EVERY COMBAT SOLDIER carries inside a repository of sights, sounds, smells, and emotions. These comprise a database of thoughts and feelings of an intensity unknown to civilians. A combat survivor returns home changed and often with a very different persona. Again, civilians are clueless about the internal metamorphosis of the returning warrior. It's not their fault. They lack a context broad enough—or grotesque enough—to conceive the internalized struggle that shapes the combat soldier psyche.

When encountering a veteran in a social setting, a civilian will offer a sincere "Thank you for your service." To which the combat soldier may find no adequate reply. The floodgates contain unspeakable thoughts, smells, and images, but just barely. Briefly, they contemplate the disconnect between the "thank you" and their response options. Depending upon the time elapsed since being in-country, the soldier will find this encounter relatively more or less of a challenge.

But, at some point—often after many years—the combat soldier becomes aware of a desire to speak of their experiences. Maybe it's a sense of urgency at the thought of losing their legacy. Or, perhaps, it's just time to "let someone in" on what *really* happened "back in the day." In any case, civilians must encourage this long latent and slow-to-emerge desire to share about something incomprehensible in the civilian world. In short, soldiers need to speak, and *we* need to hear them.

In the Summer of 2020, I engaged my older brother regarding his Vietnam experience. When I contacted him, I had no idea if he would be willing to share details from such an emotional time five decades ago. However, time waits for no one. I felt that the moment was right to ask for his first-person account as an American soldier in wartime—before it was too late and the story was lost forever.

Intensely aware of the gulf between our American experiences, I can only say to my brother, *"Thank you for your service."*

"You can kill 10 of my men for every one we kill of yours. But even at those odds, you will lose, and we will win." —Ho Chi Minh

PART-I | CONFLICT

The Numbers Game

I DISTINCTLY REMEMBER the body counts.

With the Vietnam War in full swing, nightly news anchors for the "big three" *(ABC, CBS, NBC)* solemnly shared the daily kill count for enemy and American soldiers. Even now, more than 50 years later, I clearly remember that surrealistic scorecard, and I recall that, invariably, the number of enemy combatants killed exceeded that of our troops.

With villages and territory captured incongruent in the Vietnam engagement, the American military strategy—to kill more of the enemy than they kill of us—only renders Minh's words more chilling. In a prolonged and bloody game of numbers, "Uncle Ho" understood that simply running out the clock would deliver victory to him.

From 1965 onward, that "clock" was American public sentiment ticking down like a timebomb soon to explode in violent civil unrest on college campuses and in the streets—events dutifully recorded by the media for nightly broadcast on the six- and eleven o'clock news. In the era before cell phones and the internet, the media shaped domestic perceptions of reality at home and abroad. Vietnam may not have been the first war in which embedded journalists played a vital role in capturing events on film. But, it was the first time that war coverage from the East became the catalyst for wholesale societal upheaval in the West.

Falling Between The Cracks

ALTHOUGH WE NEVER TALKED about the proverbial elephant in the room, as high school sophomores in 1972, my contemporaries and I realized that the Vietnam conflict was lingering. With the lottery draft system still in place, our thought bubbles concealed the all-important question: *Will the war continue long enough for us to get drafted?* Possibly. But, it was a reality that distracted us little from our trivial pursuits of ball games, dances, pep rallies, and parties.

By the time the Class of 1975 graduated, America had divested itself of the responsibility for containing the tumbling dominoes of communism in Southeast Asia. The requirement for registration with Selective Service and the draft itself had ended. We became a generation that fell through the cracks between World War II, Korea, and Vietnam, and the Gulf Wars just over the horizon line.

Call us *The Luckiest Generation.*

Still, some of us enlisted in the military right after graduation, and, for many, it was a good experience. Some even made careers out of their service and were eventually deployed to Grenada, Kuwait, Iraq, and Afghanistan. Along the way, enlistees grew up faster, learned more about life in a context outside of the United States, and earned ribbons and medals for courage. So, while lucky, ours is not a generation lacking bravery or patriots.

A Silent Goodbye

MY OLDER BROTHER, ROGER, signed up for ARMY ROTC during college—a wise strategy for an early Baby Boomer in the Vietnam era. Graduation from the program ensured he would enter the military as an officer leading a platoon rather than as a Private walking point in a rice paddy 9,000 miles from home. In 1970, fresh from college, my brother deployed to Vietnam at age 23.

I remember feeling conflicted over his departure. On the one hand, I knew Rog would be well-trained by the Army before arriving in-country. On the other hand, there were those bloody nightly body counts. It was difficult to contemplate his imminent fate without figuratively wallpapering over the latter with the former, a troubling exercise in probabilities for a 12-year-old.

As we lingered on the driveway of my parent's home, I found that I could not put words to my feelings at this ominous parting. As the moment came for him to get into the car for the drive to the airport, I pulled a small jack-knife from my pants pocket and gave it to him *(for protection)*. He took the knife, but I do not recall anything said between us. A lump in my throat conspired against a verbal goodbye, so we hugged, and then he was gone.

A Need to Know

MY EARLIEST MEMORIES of the 1960s were of a crowded kitchen—five kids plus mom and dad—where dinner time was always a noisy adventure. Given the decade difference between my older brother and me, he was my earliest hero, mostly because he played football for the *La Habra Highlanders* on Friday nights in the fall. At age six, I could think of nothing more fantastic than the giant boys in blue and white with enormous shoulders, shiny helmets, and three-quarter-inch spikes knocking each other about.

I saw my first *Highlander* game on a late summer night in 1963. Before I was old enough to attend the games, I remember hearing the drumline cadence wafting across the night air from the stadium a mile away from our house. With an open window and the breeze just right, the excitement of Friday night football was as near as my ear as I drifted off to sleep. Football has remained a mythical siren call to me throughout my life. On the road in any town, spotting stadium light standards within the cityscape gives me a *"There's Carmen San Diego!"* type of thrill.

As an eleven-year-old, when I donned my first football uniform for a Junior All-American team, my brother served as an assistant coach and helped teach me the game. My father and brother taught me about winning and losing, the latter lesson being a magnitude of order more critical than the former. Not long after that season ended, my brother traded his coach's whistle for an officer's sidearm and, in the blink of an eye, was whisked halfway around the world and into a giant question mark.

It had been on my heart for several years to ask my brother about his experience as a young soldier in Vietnam. As veterans often require decades before being willing to revisit such memories, much less talk about them, I wanted to allow my brother time and space to review that part of his journey and share whatever he was determined to retrieve. I provided him with a list of questions and an open-ended timeline for returning his input—*if* he chose to return it to me.

He did, and what follows is his response to my inquiry from the Summer of 2020.

PART-II | IN COUNTRY

To Vietnam and Back Again

QUESTION 1: WHEN DID you arrive in-country, how old were you, and what were your rank and first assignment?

At age 22, I entered active duty as a Second Lieutenant (2LT) in September 1969. I received several months of training: Infantry officer basic training, Airborne school, and Ranger Survival school at Fort Benning, Georgia, before reaching my first assignment with the First Armored Division, Fort Hood, Texas. I deployed to Vietnam as a 23-year-old in the Fall of 1970.

QUESTION 2: What was the social and political climate in the U.S. and abroad when you began your Vietnam experience?

By the time I entered active duty, much of the 1960s—especially from 1965 onward—had seen an explosion of public dissatisfaction with our involvement in Vietnam. Several notable politicians were regularly and loudly speaking out publicly against the war, and significant anti-war marches, populated by young draft-age students, were common. Media coverage of those marches kept the issue of the war in the public's eye, as did the airing of combat film footage showing the devastation in Vietnamese cities and villages. Particularly impactful was the regular footage showing wounded and dead American soldiers being airlifted from battlefields while narrators emphasized the number of U.S. dead and wounded. So, the political atmosphere was highly volatile, and violence during anti-war protests was seemingly the norm.

QUESTION 3: As a young man, what were your gut feelings and emotions about the situation unfolding in your life as you prepared to ship out?

As a young man with idealized notions of my patriotic duty to serve my country, I was proud to serve in the Army. Still, I had some reservations about walking voluntarily into the dangers inherent in a combat zone. At that time, TV news constantly broadcast reminders of one of the possible outcomes—and not a comforting one. So, there was some apprehension about facing the results of my decision to enter military service. But I had made a commitment and was, at that point, focused on keeping it.

QUESTION 4: How did your family, friends, and acquaintances feel about your decision to enlist?

My family supported my military service but were perhaps a bit leery of my heading to Vietnam. I don't recall experiencing anything in my interactions with them that betrayed their fear for my safety (except for mom, of course). I'm sure it was on everyone's mind as it was on mine. Looking back, I don't recall many conversations about my upcoming combat assignment. It was as though no one wanted to discuss it because it would raise the possibility that I might return much differently than I had left—or not return at all. So, there was an "ignorance is bliss" mindset with everyone. I recall that I was not interested in discussing my upcoming departure either.

QUESTION 5: What were you thinking about en route to Vietnam, and how long did it take to get there?

The journey to Vietnam began at Los Angeles International Airport with a commercial flight to Seattle-Tacoma Airport. Aircraft were unavailable at SEATAC (scheduling issues), so Flying Tiger Airlines paid for a hotel for everyone scheduled to fly to Vietnam. The next day, I boarded a military contract flight on Flying Tiger Airlines that took me and several hundred other military personnel on the first leg to Anchorage, Alaska, where we deplaned for a short period during refueling. The next leg of the journey took us to Yokota Air Base, Japan, where we stretched our legs in the terminal area while the plane refueled. The last leg of the journey brought us to Cam Ranh Bay, Vietnam. The trip, lasting over 21 hours, was somewhat exhausting.

*But through it all, I kept wondering what it would be like. Not just who I would meet but what the soldiers in my platoon would be like. Would they trust me coming in as a "new guy" (in slang FNG, or, F***ing New Guy) and an officer to boot? Had my training truly prepared me to be an officer in a combat infantry platoon? Would the combat experience mirror what I had seen in war movies, or would it be more like the mind-numbing visual news reports televised over the previous five years?*

Most of all, I wondered whether I would measure up as a leader, responsible for the lives of my soldiers who had families (as I did) anxiously awaiting their safe return from a place and a situation they could not comprehend. My most dreaded thought—more so than for my fate—was that I would make a mistake in judgment during enemy contact that would get some of my men killed or wounded.

What would I write to their parents, girlfriends, or wives? If I survived the error, how would the members of my platoon react? And how would I view myself?

Sleeping during the flights was difficult, given the unknowns racing through my mind. There was a lot of conversation around me—sports, family, a mish-mash of subjects other than Vietnam and the war. Everyone knew something about what lay ahead, but it was almost like a general unspoken agreement existed that no one should mention our destination—perhaps to avoid a "jinx" on our futures. If we did not talk about Vietnam, we would not have to think about it. And Vietnam did not exist.

Until we landed.

QUESTION 6: Can you describe your first 24 hours/30 days in-country?

First 24 Hours: We deplaned at Cam Ranh Bay air base. The place was impressive, and during the landing, it seemed like we were on final approach forever. I recall looking out the aircraft window and seeing an endless array of combat/combat support equipment spread out in orderly sections with perpendicular roadways arranged in perfect squares for easy access. Just before the plane landed, we passed over acres of pallets of Pabst Blue Ribbon *beer sitting in the sun. I remember thinking it strange to see so much beer in a combat zone. I found out later that the beer was for use in protected "rear" areas in officer and NCO clubs (as much as rear areas could exist in an unconventional war with no front lines). For sure, beer never made it to my unit in the field—which I count as a good thing.*

I remember distinctly the moment the aircraft door opened. I could almost see the humidity rolling through the opening and flowing down the aisle like an invisible tsunami. Even though it was early October, the beginning of monsoon season, it was a hot, sunny day. When the humidity hit me, it was like inhaling liquid fire. At first, it was hard to breathe and took some getting used to, and I felt my energy drain away. I quickly learned an important lesson in acclimating to Vietnam: Walk slow. And knowing where we just landed, who would want to walk fast?

After debarking at Cam Ranh Bay Air Base, I went to the 22nd Replacement Detachment for in-country processing. I proceeded through customs and received the necessary equipment, including jungle fatigues—a blessing in that they were lightweight and well-suited to the climate. My first assignment was with the 173rd Airborne Brigade.

First 30 Days: *We traveled from Cam Ranh Bay north to Phu Cat Air Base and then onto Phu Tai to in-process at 173rd Airborne Brigade headquarters. The next day, we traveled by truck to Cha Rang Valley camp for "in-country" training, all part of our acclimatization. We had classes on Medivac (Medical evacuation) procedures, field sanitation, first aid, dental hygiene, North Vietnamese (NVA) and Viet Cong (VC) combat, and sapper (infiltration) tactics and techniques. I fired several weapons for familiarity—the M-16 rifle, M-60 machine gun, M-79 20mm grenade launcher, and .50 caliber machine gun—and even threw hand grenades and operated a flame thrower.*

Because we were near the coast, the rain came nearly every day, and it was a bone-chilling rain colder than any I had ever experienced. That surprised me because of my preconception of the climate in Vietnam. The inclement weather stopped helicopter operations, so several of us—junior officers—were put in the open bed of a 2.5-ton truck and driven back to Phu Cat Air Base, where we stayed a week until the weather cleared. From there, we again headed out by military truck on Highway QL1 to my assigned unit (at the time, QL1 was the only permanently improved highway running north-to-south. It was closed at the border between North and South Vietnam).

I arrived at my unit—Company A, 4th Battalion, 503rd Infantry, 173rd Airborne Brigade—where I completed in-processing and received tactical/combat issue gear (helmet, .45 caliber pistol, and M-16 rifle with spare magazines, bayonet, flak vest, rigid rucksack, entrenching tool, poncho, pup tent with stakes and tie down line). After several days of waiting out monsoon rains, I arrived at Company A's location and met the company commander, a no-nonsense, hardened former Marine.

QUESTION 7: Can you describe your first experience on patrol?

I met the platoon sergeant (Sergeant First Class). Unfortunately for me, he was on his way to a new assignment. I then met the four squad leaders and the rest of the platoon. Fortunately, Staff Sergeant (SSG) Taylor, the next senior noncommissioned officer with experience, became my platoon sergeant—for which I was very thankful. He was professional and experienced, and I learned a lot from him in the following months.

The authorized strength for my infantry platoon was 42 soldiers. On day one, I found out I had 22 soldiers, including my squad leaders, and never had more than 30 during my tour of duty. The next day, I received an operations order (OPORD) to move out on a mission with my platoon. I barely knew any of the men now under my command and already had to lead them on a mission. Fear surfaced at the prospect of commanding soldiers whom I did not know and who did not know me. I was sure they were wondering about my leadership ability and tactical training and whether they could trust me. I thought about their willingness to obey orders from a new guy with life and death hanging in the balance. I hoped I would make the correct decisions and give the appropriate orders during enemy contact when it came to that.

We boarded UH-1 Huey helicopters for an airlift to Firebase Shamrock, an artillery position atop a mountain near the Cambodian border. The mission was to move southeast, setting up day observation posts and night ambushes over five days. The mountains comprised thick jungle, compliments of the heavy annual rainfall. Since we were working the eastern slopes, we were directly in the path of the monsoon rainstorms that quickly rolled across the flat rice paddies from the ocean. Frequent torrential rains, heavier and colder than I had ever experienced, started early in the mission and lasted several days. We were miserable.

QUESTION 8: Can you describe your first contact with the enemy?

My first encounter with the enemy was from a distance. On the first night of my first mission, we set up an ambush position on a mountainside with a clear view of a valley leading northwest and the flat terrain that stretched eastward toward the ocean several kilometers in the distance. At about 10:00 p.m., we spotted a group of 11 Viet Cong (VC) walking along rice paddy dikes about 800 meters out. We observed them using our Night Vision equipment (called Starlight Scopes). They carried two Rocket Propelled Grenade (RPG) launchers and AK-47 automatic rifles. Two or three of them wore the pith-type helmet often worn by North Vietnamese soldiers.

We were close to the maximum range of our M-60 machine gun, too far to fire on them accurately. Engaging would have revealed our location and forced us to reposition in the dark, needlessly endangering my men. I called in for helicopter gunship support, artillery support, and even heavy mortar support. The requests were denied, allegedly because of target proximity to villages designated as "friendly" to U.S. forces. After the mission, I discovered that the unit that received my encoded fire support requests incorrectly decoded the map grid coordinates and erroneously placed my requested target close to friendly villages. Sometime later, my coordinates were reevaluated and found to comply with proximity limits and appropriate for fire support. It was a very frustrating experience.

QUESTION 9: Was there an impactful experience that still affects you today?

I left Cha Rang Valley camp with several other soldiers—mostly junior officers with a couple of enlisted men—to Phu Cat Air Base in an open-top 2.5-ton truck. It had rained hard just before we departed, and water had puddled along both sides of the roadway.

Still, lots of people were out walking, heading to local village marketplaces along the road. Two other officers joined me as I stood in the cargo area, just behind the truck cab.

As the truck moved along the narrow, curbless road, we noticed the driver (an enlisted soldier) would periodically maneuver the truck close to the side of the road. We observed that he did so when Vietnamese people were close to puddles of muddy water. It was evident that he was trying to splash them. Once, we looked back and saw some women and children drenched with water and two other kids lying on the ground. We immediately pounded on the canvas top of the truck cab and yelled at the driver to stop doing this. We later reported him to authorities at Phu Cat Air Base.

This incident greatly impacted me as it revealed how easily war can lead us to dehumanize combatants and civilians alike, resulting in inhumane treatment by U.S. soldiers. I have always remembered that experience when dealing with others since that time. It was a lesson that war can turn even a "nice guy" into someone unworthy of emulation.

QUESTION 10: How did your first encounter with death in-country impact you?

My platoon was on a sweep mission in search of enemy soldiers. We came upon a small encampment riddled with rocket fire. It was a stark scene with branchless trees, deep impact craters, and almost no ground-level vegetation. At various places in the camp, my platoon and I came upon the deceased: An elderly man at the entrance of a small cave, two young women and two small children out in the open, and another man who appeared to be on a makeshift medical table as if he had been receiving treatment at the time of the attack. None of the bodies showed evidence of obvious trauma; they looked like they were sleeping. The scene seemed surreal.

We covered the victims with cloth material found at the site and no-tified headquarters of our findings. The image of those children has remained with me ever since. It seemed unreal that they were there. They should have been off somewhere in a village, perhaps playing soccer with friends. As a 23-year-old, I struggled to process the real-ity of that moment. My thoughts wandered to images of children in America who were safely playing with friends, unafraid of ground or air attacks or soldiers raiding their homes and towns.

QUESTION 11: How did your worldview change during your months in-country?

During my time in Vietnam, 1970-71, I remained committed to what I felt was a worthwhile cause. But I did not give much thought to my worldview. I focused heavily on my responsibility for being a good leader and keeping my men and myself alive while carrying out our assigned missions. So, changes to my worldview were slow to come while I was preoccupied with keeping my men and myself alive. Those kinds of changes would come later.

QUESTION 12: Who were some memorable fellow troops and what was notable about them, and the experiences you shared?

Two men stand out: Private First-Class Boulder and Specialist 4 Robinson.

PFC Boulder was unforgettable because of his stature. He was about 6'2", muscular, and a quiet guy. He seemed never to tire when he was the point man for the platoon traveling through dense jungle, which happened often. We tried to stay off existing trails as they were frequently boobie-trapped (the equivalent of the Gulf War's IED). Boulder swung a mighty machete through jungle vines and vegetation—like a hot knife through butter. And when his machete needed help, he pushed his body through the thick jungle growth like a bulldozer.

Specialist 4 Robinson, on the other hand, was the tiniest soldier in the platoon, maybe 5'6". His nickname was "Little Bit." However, in addition to his rifle/ammunition in his rucksack, he made it his mission to carry more grenades and extra machine gun ammunition than anyone else. When asked why he hauled so much extra ammunition, Robinson just smiled. He said he didn't want the platoon to run out. We never could quite figure out whether Robinson was supernaturally strong or just ran on adrenaline all the time. He had a great smile and happy-go-lucky attitude, which was amazing to see in the middle of a combat zone.

QUESTION 13: What were some impactful mistakes made and lessons learned?

One lesson learned during my Vietnam tour of duty pertains to strategy at the level of our national government. There were many restrictions on when we could respond with force and the criteria for doing so—both at the combat unit and theater commander levels. It felt like we were trying to achieve the stated goal of fighting the spread of communism in Vietnam and Southeast Asia with one hand tied behind our backs. The rules of engagement seemed con-

trary to the maxim that to defeat the enemy, hit them hard with the force needed to win and then keep the pressure on. The strategic disconnect caused frustration on more than one occasion.

On a personal level, I remember that at the end of my first patrol, I did not account for the impact of the heavy rainfall on the lowland terrain we would have to cross. Had we left earlier, we would have avoided being trapped by the confluence of several rain-swollen streams flowing too swiftly to cross safely. Consequently, my platoon had to take shelter in an abandoned village most likely familiar to enemy soldiers—a static and vulnerable position. Fortunately, the rain abated quickly, and the water levels fell faster than expected. We minimized our exposure to discovery by enemy forces and exited the area post haste. Lesson learned.

QUESTION 14: How do emotions and feelings impact a soldier in the field?

The cycle of emotions was very intense. There were days between missions when we were busy cleaning weapons, writing letters to loved ones, and catching as much sleep as possible before the next task. But, always present in the back of all our minds was the sense that, at any moment, there could be an enemy attack. It could come on the ground or through mortar or rocket fire with little warning before the first explosion. So, even during downtimes, we were always alert for danger.

When the order came to move out on a mission, adrenaline levels skyrocketed. As we prepared for a search-and-destroy mission to disrupt enemy activities, take prisoners for questioning, and eliminate enemy weapon/food supply caches, a constant train of thought ran through our heads: Will this be my last mission? Will I react in time to protect my own life and the lives of my comrades? Will I make it back home?

It was a rollercoaster of adrenaline highs interspersed with hours of downtime for equipment maintenance. Each soldier's Vietnam tour of duty was an exhausting year-long exercise in stress containment. As a soldier closed in on his scheduled return to the U.S., a battle ensued with fear and paranoia. No one wanted to die on a mission just before their assigned return to the States.

Once, our platoon received orders to move 15 kilometers to set up as a blocking force for other units (U.S. and Korean). We had just dug in on a ridgeline when we got an emergency order giving us two hours to relocate to another position. The reason? A scheduled B-52 bombing mission near our location. We needed to put as much distance as possible between us and the designated target area.

We all had seen evidence of what a multiplane B-52 bombing raid could do, so we were in an elevated emotional state, wanting to move quickly while not ignoring the possible presence of the enemy along our path of movement. We made it outside the danger zone, but we could still feel the concussion effect of the bombs hitting the ground. In addition to being tired from the rapid 12-kilometer jaunt through mountainous jungle terrain, we were all a little angry.

No one in higher authority had communicated air attack plans with the ground commanders. Due to a breakdown in tactical and strategic planning, our initial order unnecessarily endangered my unit—another very frustrating experience.

QUESTION 15: How did the Vietnam experience change your view of America, its leaders, and your military chain of command?

When I arrived in Vietnam, I was onboard with—and committed to—the raison d'être given for the U.S. presence there: To combat the spread of communism to South Vietnam and beyond. After experiencing the restrictions on U.S. forces down to the platoon level and observing the social climate during my college years (1966-69), I became convinced that our political leaders were more interested in appeasing peace demonstrators to avoid political losses at home. In addition to piecemeal mobilization of forces sent to/from Vietnam, announcing deployments/redeployments in advance was, in my mind, like General Eisenhower sending a message to Adolf Hitler detailing the date and time of the Normandy invasion.

One of our Nation's Constitutional protections places the military command under civilian control. Our generals cannot simply wake up one morning and decide to invade a randomly chosen country designated by a red pin on a map. On the other hand, I perceived our political leaders would not fully commit to strategic input from experienced military leaders. Over time, it appeared that the original enthusiasm to fight communism in Vietnam morphed into an exercise in trying not to lose the war in an obvious way—and to save face. All at the expense of American soldiers.

I maintain that the U.S. is a just nation concerned with—and committed to—helping people suffering under oppressive regimes. However, determining which foreign governments to support, the specific types of aid provided, and the methods for rendering that aid requires wisdom. The fundamental question is this: Are we helping prop up an oppressive regime, or will our assistance make a positive difference in the lives of a nation's people? Lastly, the efficacy of any assistance provided will depend on its acceptance by the populace (not just their government) and their understanding of any conditions attached to the aid rendered.

QUESTION 16: What was your impression of the Vietnamese people from encounters with them?

The Vietnamese people seemed peaceful and agreeable, at least the people I met while on patrol. My platoon had a Vietnamese interpreter to communicate with local villagers while we were on missions. It was a bit nerve-wracking during the questioning of the local populace because we were never sure that the answers translated for us were accurate regarding the proximity of enemy soldiers in our area of operation. We never encountered a problem traced back to mistranslation, intentional or otherwise.

One critical challenge of the Vietnam War was adjusting to cultural differences in interpersonal exchanges. Entering Vietnam, I received a U.S. State Department booklet that explained some of the cultural disparities between America and Vietnam. A subtle but significant difference was that the Vietnamese people believe it to be a sign of disrespect to make direct eye contact with someone—particularly an elder, someone in authority, or a casual acquaintance. Hence, it was difficult to determine whether answers to our questions about enemy activity in our patrol areas were truthful. Given that cultural difference alone, it was easy to see how trust was hard to build between U.S. soldiers and Vietnamese citizens. The fact that our military began to be viewed by many as an "occupying force" probably didn't engender much trust from the local population sandwiched between our operations during the day and those of the Viet Cong at night.

Ironically, much later, I would spend 21 years as a middle and high school Physical Education and Health teacher, sports coach, and mentor. During that time, I had a lot of foreign exchange students in my classes, many of them from Vietnam. I got to know them very well in class and through my coaching and mentoring duties. Over time, contact with them built within me a more positive view of Vietnamese people. I found my students courageous in leaving their homes behind to live in America—some with limited English skills—and to work hard to learn and achieve everything they could in American schools.

My experiences gave me an even greater appreciation of the similarities between me and my foreign exchange students. These kids hailed from Vietnam, South Korea, Japan, Taiwan, and Mexico, giving me a multicultural experience I am glad for. And, years after my combat tour of duty in Vietnam, connecting with Vietnamese students in a different setting was a special blessing that I could not have anticipated—one I am grateful for. To this day, I follow the achievements of my students as they move on to university-level studies and challenging jobs.

QUESTION 17: What were the last 30 days in-country like prior to your return to America?

During the final 30 days of my tour, our unit relocated to the Saigon area and prepared to ship out to the U.S. The 173rd Airborne Brigade was designated to stand down and return to the U.S.

to become the 3rd Brigade of the 101st Airborne Division at Ft. Campbell, Kentucky. There was a lot of work to do to preserve and pack all manner of equipment and vehicles not designated for other units in-country or handed off to the South Vietnamese Army.

At this point, though there was always the possibility of attack anywhere in Vietnam—infiltrators with bombs, rockets, or mortars—I relaxed a little, envisioned the lights of home on the horizon, and realized that I would most likely make it back to the U.S. I experienced no significant enemy actions during this time. Perhaps this was because our government had announced that units would withdraw on a set timetable. Maybe the enemy felt no need to press military actions as it was evident that the U.S. would eventually be gone.

And, by 1973, we were.

QUESTION 18: We hear a lot about how Vietnam vets were "received" upon their return to the U.S. What was your specific experience?

When I left Vietnam to return to the U.S., I knew little about how the public's reactions to the war had progressed from the late 1960s forward. Very few soldiers had regular access to the Stars and Stripes *newspaper printed in Vietnam or* Armed Forces Radio *broadcasts. But I was not prepared for how much more aggressive the anti-war movement had become. I had no idea how much anger towards those who served in the military had grown during my year in Vietnam. This anger was misdirected at the soldiers, sailors, Marines, and airmen because we went to Vietnam at the direction of the civilian politicians who established strategic policy affecting the use of our military to support national goals.*

The ever-growing unpopularity of the Vietnam War during the 1960s prompted many angry and often violent public demonstrations. Out-of-control emotional reactions between opposing groups led to increased hate speech that divided Americans along socioeconomic, political, racial, and religious lines. Things had deteriorated to the point that when I returned to the U.S., there were no welcoming parades, no accolades for a job done well, and no positive recognition whatsoever. The attitude of most Americans I encountered upon returning was either to ignore me (and my experience) or to express open hostility towards me physically and verbally.

Returning to the U.S., I departed from Tan Son Nhut Airbase (Saigon) and flew into Travis Air Force Base in California rather than McChord AFB in Washington. Travis was closer to my home in La Habra, California. At that time, there were very few convenient flights from Sacramento to Los Angeles, so I and several other officers took a cab to San Francisco International Airport. As we were anxious to return home, we did not think about changing out of our uniforms (required for travel on military contract flights).

We were in for a shock!

It was a long walk through the terminal at SFO to the departure gate. The experience was like running a gauntlet—only we had to walk. Along the way, we were abused by more people than we could count. They called us "baby killers" and other epithets, and some people even threw drink cartons at us or spat in our direction. We knew we dared not respond as it was clear that the antagonists were trying to get us to react inappropriately. Worse still, the rest of the people in the terminal—our fellow citizens—remained spectators, just sitting there, saying nothing, doing nothing. That hurt as much as the hateful, open hostility of those who showed no appreciation for our service.

QUESTION 19: Looking back, what is important to you about your Vietnam experience?

I believe that the experience helped me to become more at ease with myself and to understand that I could make critical decisions that impacted people other than myself. The latter, in particular, was a big realization compared to my mindset before going to Vietnam. Over the years, this newfound confidence helped me more effectively deal with adults and young people. As a result of my Vietnam experience, I also learned not to prejudge or develop preconceived ideas about people or nations before knowing anything about them.

QUESTION 20: If you could spend 10 minutes with the 23-year-old Roger about to ship out for Vietnam, what would you share with him?

I would tell Roger-23 to be more confident in himself and the training received at Ft. Benning, Georgia, and Ft. Sherman, Panama Canal Zone.

When I deployed, I believed in God and considered myself a Christian. But, years later, I realized that I had not fully committed myself to following Jesus. In retrospect, had my faith been stronger back then, I would have been better able to deal with the fear and ap-

prehension of going to war and being a leader whose actions could mean the difference between life and death for the men under my command.

Also, greater confidence and stronger faith would have benefitted my family relationships after I returned home. Had my faith in God been stronger back then, much of the fear, doubt, and stress that plagued me would have diminished during difficult times.

QUESTION 21: You received the Purple Heart medal for wounds suffered in battle. What happened and what were your thoughts about receiving the medal?

I was a platoon leader for the 4.2-inch mortar platoon of Company E, 4th Battalion, 173rd Airborne Brigade. We held a position on a small mountaintop on the eastern side of the range, with a clear view of the rice fields stretching several miles to the ocean. We were the protection for our Battalion Commander and his field staff. May 22, 1971, dawned like any other day, heat and humidity spiking together to let us all know that nothing would be different from the day before.

I had just left my bunker to do a morning check on my soldiers in their fighting positions and to watch my three 4.2-inch mortar crews prepare for dry fire mission training. As I completed my inspection and headed toward my bunker, I heard an explosion about twenty feet down the slope from me. It took only a second or two to realize that our position was under mortar attack, but it seemed longer. I was several feet away from the only close cover, the mortar ammunition bunker with its uncompleted protective roof. So, I dove into that pit containing 350 High Explosive (HE) mortar rounds and 100+ Phosphorus rounds.

As I dove into the ammo pit, two more explosions occurred—much closer to me than the first one. I felt something penetrate my left foot just before I hit the ground. I checked and saw that I was bleeding from a wound just above my left knee and on the top of my foot. My 4.2-inch mortar gunners quickly figured out the direction of the fire and responded with multiple rounds, silencing the enemy mortar crew. The enemy landed about a dozen 82 mm mortar rounds within our perimeter, including two CS-type gas rounds. Our platoon radio operator was the only casualty (KIA) other than myself.

Our medic treated my wounds while we awaited a UH-1 medevac helicopter. Because we had just received fire, the helicopter pilot hesitated to land and became vulnerable to possible enemy fire. Eventually, when he touched down, several of my soldiers placed me onboard for a trip to the medical facility at Landing Zone English.

My wounds consisted of small pieces of shrapnel above the left knee and in my left foot. Fortunately, the pieces did not penetrate deeply. Doctors held me for observation to ensure there was no infection. They wanted to keep me for about a week but agreed to release me after two days as I wanted to be back with my platoon.

The mortar attack happened very quickly. And it's true: During a traumatic event, things seem to move in slow motion. I didn't have time to think, so my reaction to the event was instinctive—the result of my training. Later, during treatment at LZ English, I had time *to reflect on not being more severely injured. I was to meet my wife in Hawai'i for a week's R&R in June, so receiving relatively minor injuries was a blessing.*

The medical facility submitted the request for the Purple Heart through channels at brigade headquarters. I received the Purple Heart medal and certificate when I returned to LZ English after my R&R in Hawai'i. It was a small ceremony which suited me fine. I recall looking at the medal in the presentation box and thinking that the events of May 22 seemed like ancient history instead of merely a month ago. I returned to my platoon and didn't give much thought to the Purple Heart.

When I was at Tan Son Nhut airport in Saigon, awaiting my flight home at the end of my tour of duty, a couple of administrative duty soldiers commented on the Purple Heart ribbon on my uniform. I felt a little awkward that they pointed it out. But later, after reading a book about the origin of the Purple Heart medal, its history, and some notable recipients (many of whom received the award posthumously), I gained a greater appreciation for what it means to those wounded in service to America. From that point onward, wearing it on my uniform became more of an honor, with reverence toward those many servicemen/women who received their PH medal under deadlier circumstances than what I faced.

Years ago, I joined the Military Order of the Purple Heart, an organization made up solely of PH medal recipients and dedicated to promoting patriotism, supporting legislative initiatives, and helping our military veterans. Over the years, I have gained a greater appreciation for the Purple Heart medal.

We Regret to Inform You

IN A GRAINY INTERNALIZED snapshot, I remember the day the telegram arrived. *Western Union.* My parents never let me read the text, but the impact was the same for all of us. In that horrifying moment, we did not realize that a telegram was good news. Had my brother's status been KIA instead of WIA, soldiers would have delivered the bad news to our doorstep in person. Still, this was an emotionally charged moment without precedent in our lives.

For years afterward, I wondered what had happened to my brother in that strange land on the other side of the globe. I never asked, and he never told me. It was not as if I didn't want to understand the soldier's experience in Vietnam. To be shot at. To be wounded. But I respected my brother's right to peace and silence. By the time he returned to the States, the popularity of Vietnam vets hovered somewhere near that of Hollywood "Commies" in the 1950s.

Even now, nearly half a century after my brother's time in-country, I hesitated to ask him to fill in the blanks about a time, place, and events he might prefer to avoid thinking about. Only my brother could shed light on a complex and troubling period in American history from the perspective of the first-born son of our family. I found that I needed that information. So, I asked him for it. Graciously, he was willing to provide it.

PART-III | RETROSPECTIVE

With Eyes Wide Open

QUESTION 22: HOW DID the Vietnam War change you and what perspectives are essential for civilians to understand?

My participation in the Vietnam War did bring about some changes in my mindset. In retrospect, I see that—aside from the perceived shunning by American society that I and other Vietnam veterans received—I was reluctant to speak about my feelings and the war itself. Privately, I questioned my motives for even serving in the military. I wrestled with the patriotic pride that I took with me to war and the realities of our very presence in a country whose everyday citizens saw us as an occupying force and not as saviors. Most Vietnamese people (outside of the political/governmental power structure) were trying to live and raise families like most people strive to—except they had to do so while walking a tightrope between U.S. forces/allies and our determined enemies. Their existence must have been a roller coaster of fear for their lives and those of their children.

I must admit that I and other Vietnam vets experienced a loss of faith in—and even a sense of betrayal by—our political leaders. They sent us to fight for a cause we believed in and stated that the cause—to deter the spread of communism in Asia—was just. Yet, in the end, the hands of the military were tied by the political games-

manship in Washington, D.C. From the senior ground force commanders to battalion, company, and platoon levels, the rules of engagement changed as often as the ocean tide.

In retrospect, I could not detect a clear-cut plan for victory and withdrawal after a "declared win." Even with a plan, Vietnam was an unconventional war. There were no delineated front lines or rear areas. There was no territory to capture and clear of enemy combatants. There was no plan for declaring "victory" and exiting the battlefield. Vietnam was a war we could not "win."

During the war, the consistent message from the generals and politicians was "We are making progress" (purportedly toward that eventual victory). Over time, I realized that our effort was not unlike trying to kill a gnat with a sledgehammer. Amazingly, the world's most powerful military was stuck in a war with no face-saving way out, no end in sight, and with ever-escalating political upheaval at home.

It was a heartbreaking realization that as we left Vietnam, we would have to contemplate metaphorical thought bubbles over a sea of white crosses and Stars of David, hauntingly asking, "What was it all for?"

I gave my all in Vietnam, and it hurt to return to an ungrateful nation and a silent reception that virtually screamed, "No one cares!" Except that we were no longer "over there." America seemed more focused on forgetting about the war as quickly as possible.

It took a few years before I could reconcile the truth of our doomed crusade for "freedom" with its initial good intentions. In a way, I still think our collective hearts were in the right place, given our pri-

mary desire to help the South Vietnamese people. However, democratic ideals are best implemented and defended if the citizens of a nation are personally committed to instituting the change from autocracy to democracy. The forced implementation of a sovereign nation's polity model from the outside does not have much chance for success.

Still, I would fight again alongside the soldiers with whom I served back then. They were the best. We looked out for one another. In the face of possible death, we bonded like no one can understand unless they have been in a similar circumstance. There was unquestioned loyalty to the platoon and one another. Atheists were absent from our foxholes, and neither cultural nor racial differences separated us.

I often wish that society could embrace the demonstrated commitment and loyalty I experienced in Vietnam without the pall of combat as a motivator.

Moving Forward

REVIEWING THE JOURNEY from a vantage point in 2020, I know that my Vietnam experience significantly changed me. I appreciate life and the blessings of living in America to a greater degree. So many others throughout the world do not get to enjoy what we Americans have here. Out of the stressful circumstances of that year in Vietnam, I found confidence through my leadership role and working with others of different backgrounds. I learned to be more tolerant of the ethnic backgrounds, beliefs, and cultures of others.

RONALD KAYS

Seeing the Vietnamese people and observing them, even sharing a meal with village chiefs, I discerned that we have much in common despite cultural differences in our respective countries. It may seem odd, but I received many more blessings out of a year under fire in a foreign country than I thought possible. For that, I am grateful.

Roger B. Kays, Major, U.S. Army (Ret)

PART-IV | DEJA VU

Afghanistan 2021/Vietnam 1975

OVER THE PAST TWO DECADES, I have read extensively on engagements in the Afghanistan and Iraq wars. Books like *Lone Survivor* (Marcus Luttrell), *Red Platoon* (Clint Romesha), and many others vividly detail the horrors of war and the ties that bind the soldiers we send to fight in them. And when we send them, the unspoken "ask" is that they—the soldiers—do the dirty work abroad so that we, at home, remain largely unaffected by the nasty details.

But those details are deeply troubling, particularly the events of August 2021. We witnessed an ill-advised end-of-engagement and withdrawal from Afghanistan that triggered chaos, panic, and bloodshed. We can debate whether, with our original objectives met, we should have departed the region years ago *(probably)*. We can argue whether Taliban 2.0 in Afghanistan will somehow be "moderate" *(not a chance)*. But we can agree that the dysfunctionality of the U.S. Government in abandoning Afghan citizens to a cruel fate under a brutal regime revives unsettling thoughts about the closing scenes of the Vietnam conflict.

Defenders of the current President of the United States—the Commander in Chief of the U.S. Military Forces—would argue that *any* withdrawal, given similar logistics and complexities, would, of necessity, be non-optimal. Myriad political and practical considerations attend a military end-of-engagement: transitioning/destroying unused physical assets; transitioning support for in-country allies; exfiltrating U.S. citizens, military personnel, and indigenous support personnel; completing in-country infrastructure obligations.

Any way you slice it, ending a war is complicated.

Contextual differences aside, the Vietnam and Afghanistan wars ended badly for the United States military, the then-serving Commander in Chief, and citizens in the affected countries *(though for vastly different reasons).*

Regarding Vietnam, the 1973 Paris Peace Accord proved fragile and tenuous. In April 1975, some two years after the signing of the Accord, Ho Chi Minh's forces swept southward toward Saigon as American forces rigged a hasty exfiltration plan, and media and diplomatic personnel scrambled for the exits. Vietnamese citizens caught in the middle—as Afghan citizens would be in 2021—braced for the inevitable blood-letting accompanying regime change.

With two jarring end-of-engagement scenarios crippling America's domestic and international credibility, I asked my brother to compare and contrast the end of both the Vietnam and Afghanistan wars from his perspective as a Purple Heart recipient in the former.

QUESTION 23: With the August 2021 withdrawal of U.S. troops from Afghanistan and the concurrent takeover of the country by the Taliban, do you see parallels between this and the 1975 U.S. departure from Vietnam?

I see parallels between our involvement and eventual departure from Vietnam and Afghanistan.

In Vietnam, the essential mission was to prevent a so-called "domino effect" whereby nations in Asia would consecutively fall under communist control as proxies of China or the Soviet Union. Following the defeat of French forces by the Viet Minh at Dien Bien Phu in 1954, U.S. advisors deployed to assist the South Vietnamese government and armed forces. Our initial advisory role escalated gradually until the controversial Gulf of Tonkin incident provided then-president Lyndon Johnson a convenient reason to send combat troops in 1965, including naval sea/air forces and land-based air forces.

The stated mission in Afghanistan was to destroy Al Qaeda training camps and to find Osama bin Laden, the primary architect of the 9/11 attacks on the World Trade Center and Pentagon. After intelligence revealed bin Laden had fled to Pakistan, the U.S. could have ended the Afghanistan engagement. Unfortunately, then-Commander-in-Chief George W. Bush was determined to pursue the utopian vision of exporting democracy to other countries—nation-building—and helping the world become better and more peaceful.

In Vietnam, we opposed North Vietnamese Army troops and Viet Cong guerillas. In Afghanistan, we engaged the Taliban, Al Qaeda, and other extremist factions. The essential end-of-engagement disparity vis-à-vis these two wars was a factor of withdrawal execution.

Vietnam: American diplomatic representatives and North Vietnamese government officials negotiated U.S. combat operations and troop reduction and departure during the Paris Peace Accords, signed on January 27, 1973. Before the signing, then-president Richard Nixon and his NSA, Henry Kissinger, employed a lengthy process of "Vietnamization"—transitioning the burden for military execution from U.S. forces to the armed forces of the Republic of South Vietnam. This exit strategy met with mixed results as some ARVN leaders/forces performed well while others were not up to the task. Additionally, the transition suffered as South Vietnamese President Nguyen Van Thieu juggled political, social, and military objectives to retain power after the U.S. departure.

Afghanistan: While there may have been a tacit agreement between then-president Donald Trump and the Taliban for allowing a peaceful withdrawal of U.S. forces, the consequences for non-compliance were a known factor—the Taliban understood that President Trump would respond to treachery with decisive force. However, the successor administration of President Joe Biden appears to have ignored or dismissed military and intelligence advice regarding end-of-engagement imperatives for Afghanistan: protecting Bagram Air Base; evacuating U.S. citizens, NGO employees, and Afghan citizens wishing to leave; withdrawing U.S. military personnel along with any high intelligence-value equipment to prevent its appropriation by the enemy.

As I watched helicopters darting in and around Kabul in late August of 2021—the result of the Biden Administration's insufficient withdrawal planning/execution—images immediately came to mind of the helicopter evacuation of staff and local Vietnamese citizens from the U.S. Embassy roof in Saigon. But the Afghanistan exfiltration was significantly more chaotic. As the capital descended into chaos with Taliban atrocities unfolding in real-time, I felt an intense sadness. Questions that had plagued me in 1975 as I saw Saigon fall to the North Vietnamese forces came back to haunt me: "Was it all worth it? Did my comrades-in-arms die in vain?" At a time still so close to the events unfolding in Kabul, those are difficult questions to answer. But they require answers.

QUESTION 24: With those parallels in mind, do you believe there is an overarching end-of-mission strategy that could have prevented—or reduced—the calamities and atrocities that attended the U.S. departure from both countries?

Following the departure of U.S. combat troops from Vietnam in 1973, we had two years to observe the North Vietnamese and assess their compliance with the terms of the Paris Peace Accords. Therefore, we had substantially advanced warning of the impending fall of South Vietnam as communist troops continued their insurgency, Paris Accords notwithstanding. However, a war-weary Congress denied funding and troop support for the South Vietnamese government as the NVA forces crossed the DMZ and closed in on Saigon.

In Afghanistan, we had just 11 days to witness the impact of President Biden's politically symbolic but ill-advised "out by 9/11" mandate and the resulting chaotic, disorderly, and blood-soaked evacuation that subsequently destroyed the reputation of the United States as a world power and reliable ally.

In the technologically sophisticated age in which we live, the bloody details of the failed end-of-engagement strategy in Afghanistan—broadcast to the world in real-time—will embolden terrorist groups bent on destroying the West—and America in particular. Over time, the impact of the Afghanistan calamity may prove far worse than that which attended our alleged "face-saving" departure from Vietnam under the umbrella of a negotiated treaty in a world without the internet and minus a camera in every hand.

In Vietnam and Afghanistan, more thoughtful and detailed end-of-engagement planning could have changed the outcome—particularly in Afghanistan. I say 'could' because there are no guarantees in times of war. There is a saying that "the best-designed military plan never survives first contact with the enemy," primarily because too many execution-phase variables are beyond the control of strategic planners.

QUESTION 25: In Vietnam and Afghanistan, how would you apportion responsibility/blame for the failures that attended the U.S. end-of-engagement?

Extracting U.S. forces from any significant engagement requires planning at the highest level of the military—the Department of Defense (and all branch Secretaries) in coordination with the State Department and intelligence agencies (CIA, NSA, etc.). That's the starting point.

In our constitutional republic, the military is under civilian control. As Commander-in-Chief, the U.S. President gives final approval for military plans, relying on the advice of military experts who provide input as POTUS reviews the plan. So, as President Biden said repeatedly, "The buck stops here!" referring to himself.

However, President Biden shares responsibility for the chaotic withdrawal from Afghanistan with senior military commanders, the Secretary of Defense, and military branch Secretaries. Even if they warned Presidents Nixon/Ford (Vietnam) or Trump/Biden (Afghanistan)—and whether or not they sounded alarms during security briefings—the administrative and military brain trust shares responsibility for the results.

I remain in contact with many former military comrades, and we agree that the United States didn't need to be in Afghanistan for 20 years. Likewise, we are unanimous in our opinion that the end-of-engagement execution and priorities of the Biden Administration were grossly inadequate to the point of being negligent—perhaps criminally so.

Had President Biden designated a hard departure date and requested a detailed end-of-engagement plan well in advance, the State Department and DOD, working with our Allies, could have delivered a sound withdrawal strategy. At a minimum, a workable plan would have required retaining Bagram Air Base as an operations center for evacuating civilians, NGOs, select Afghan citizens, and U.S. troops and equipment.

But neither the Commander-in-Chief nor his departmental advisors and the joint chiefs of staff delivered such a plan. Hence, when Biden switched off the lights at Bagram, the nearly 5,000 enemy POWs then incarcerated at the air base were released by the Taliban.

Lastly, a detailed plan would have involved our British and Australian allies. All the President needed to do was ask his cabinet and military experts and assess their professional recommendations. Instead, Biden chose to indulge in political theater focused on getting America out of Afghanistan before the 20th anniversary of the original 9/11 attack.

In summary, the similarities between Afghanistan and Vietnam go beyond the lengthy U.S. involvement in both wars. In both, we fought wars complicated by arbitrary rules of engagement against non-traditional armed forces using guerilla tactics. In both, our political will fractured and then dissolved entirely over time. In both, we supported corrupt regimes overwhelmed by enemies propelled by nationalistic or religious ideologies and supported by third-party nations.

One differentiator in Afghanistan: Whether or not we intended it as a goal, we failed at nation-building because we didn't recognize the deeply ingrained tribalism and ancient practices permeating Afghan society. As an aside, this mistake also was made earlier in Iraq.

QUESTION 26: Having watched the end-of-engagement in Afghanistan and the chaos and deaths of both U.S. soldiers and Afghan civilians at Kabul airport, what was the most challenging duty of your Vietnam experience?

As a junior officer, extra assignments come with the job. On several occasions, I performed Survivor Assistance Officer duty (SAO) to help families deal with the loss of a son/daughter who died in combat or under other circumstances. This role required a balancing act between being sensitive to the family's loss while guiding them through myriad government regulations and forms regarding insurance coverage and payment, obtaining the decedent's back pay, etc.

I distinctly recall how difficult it was to execute my official duties and not be overwhelmed by the family's grief and emotions. The experience was like being on the beach with waves of intense feelings rolling over me instead of water. Thinking back on SAO duties, I was reminded of a time in Vietnam when I had to collect and process the personal belongings of one soldier in my platoon killed in action.

He had just returned from a 30-day leave during which he married his high school sweetheart. The company commander would not let me delay my patrol departure so this soldier could rejoin my platoon. Consequently, my soldier joined a different platoon whose Lieutenant designated him point-man. On the second day on patrol, he walked into a booby trap (IED in today's warfare). He died in the medivac helicopter 10 minutes after liftoff.

Writing letters to his parents and wife of less than a month was exceedingly difficult. He wasn't a blood relative, but he was a brother-in-arms. For many years afterward, I had a recurring dream where I saw him in silhouette but could not see his face nor recall his name. I wondered if I should have been more forceful in insisting that the company commander allow my platoon to wait for my soldier to rejoin my unit. The risk would have been my insubordination or jeopardizing the timing of our assigned mission. Several years ago, I located the incident report through Army casualty records and found this soldier's name and photo. After that, the dreams gradually faded, and I felt some relief.

PART-V | THE BEAT GOES ON

Onward Into Ukraine

THE BLOODY AND CHAOTIC U.S. withdrawal from Afghanistan in August 2021 culminated with a terrorist bombing at Kabul airport. Thirteen U.S. soldiers and over one hundred Afghan citizens perished in the blast.[1] The impact of the withdrawal—specifically, the impact of weapons and munitions left behind by the U.S. military—may be implicated in further violence as recently as October 2023.

An NSSF article on October 10, 2023, reported that weapons abandoned in Afghanistan may have made their way into the possession of Hamas terrorists during the surprise attack on Israel on October 7.[2] Previous reports estimate that the Biden regime left more than $7B in weapons and equipment in-country when the last Americans departed from *Karzai International Airport.*[3] The abandoned munitions and equipment were the ultimate low-hanging fruit and ripe for subsequent use by the Taliban and other regional players.

No sooner had the blood dried from the terrorist attack at *Hamid Karzai International Airport* than the President of the United States deemed it necessary to engage in another significant regional conflict with global implications. Ostensibly to counter the threat of a reconstituted rogue and nuclear-armed

Russia, the Biden administration began funneling money and supplies to Ukraine to support the regime of Volodymyr Zelenskyy after Russia invaded in February 2022.

For his part, Zelenskyy, a former actor, played to a sympathetic U.S. Congress, most of whom fawned over his impassioned words from the chamber floor. In contrast, Russian President Vladimir Putin remains public enemy number one inside the Beltway, in DNC circles, and within American media. As of late 2023, Zelenskyy's support in Congress has wavered some, but not enough to curtail additional massive infusions of cash and munitions from Washington.

Since the most recent conflict between Russia and Ukraine began in early 2022, the Biden administration has given nearly $113B in cash and military aid packages to Zelenskyy's regime.[4] Given Biden's persistent support of Zelenskyy and Ukraine, it seems only a matter of time before U.S. troops become part of the package. In April 2023, the *Daily Beast*[5] reported that U.S. special forces were on the ground in Ukraine.

In keeping with a long tradition of forced justification for military involvement, whether through a declaration of war or—in the case of Ukraine—by proxy, the Biden administration and the joint chiefs of staff of the military have insisted Putin's revitalized Russia is the reason for U.S. involvement in Ukraine. Stopping Putin at any cost seems to be their rationale. Even if Biden can accomplish that goal without triggering World War III, the ultimate cost will be staggering.

We've Seen This Movie Before

THE SHOW BEGINS WITH a promise of U.S. intervention "for the greater good" and continues with an extended parody of democracy-in-action. As the years go by, the bloody fingerprints of multiple presidential administrations wind up on the bodies of those sacrificed to "the cause." Billions of dollars are funneled into the gaping maw of conflict, ostensibly to "help our boys!" Then stalemate—or worse yet, quagmire. In the closing scene, head-scratching and hand-wringing accompany the ultimate predicament: *"How do we get out of here?"* As the final curtain falls, millions of eyes watch from a distance the frantic scattering of people desperately seeking a way out of the bloody kill zone.

In essence, we have another Vietnam. Or Afghanistan. Or Iraq.

PART-VI | THE VALLEY OF DECISION

America at a Crossroads

IN THE BEGINNING, THE United States of America was founded upon the biblical principle that a Creator God endowed all humanity with "certain unalienable Rights."[6] Until recently, that endowment—the right to Life, Liberty, and the Pursuit of Happiness—has been deeply embedded in the American psyche. From 2016 onward, those God-given rights have rapidly slipped through our fingers as the twin towers of Marxist socialism and speech/thought suppression overshadowed the ideals of the Founding Fathers.

The "twin towers" analogy is intentional, for the freedoms enshrined in the Declaration were dealt a lethal blow by the incorporation of the Patriot Act shortly after the 9/11 attacks in New York City, Washington, D.C., and in the skies over rural Pennsylvania. Tacitly declared as a necessary measure for fighting terrorism and forestalling future terrorist attacks on America, The Patriot Act set the stage for downstream abuses of power by agencies of the federal government tasked with enforcing its provisions.

In particular, Section 215 of the Patriot Act *(and its subsequently modified equivalent, the USA Freedom Act, 2015)*, originally in place to permit surveillance and accumulation of data to thwart foreign actors, over time became a way for federal agencies to surveil American citizens.[7] The mass accumulation of telephony metadata attached to American citizens seemed to cross into illegal search and seizure in violation of the Fourth Amendment of the U.S. Constitution.

As of this writing, aspects of the Patriot Act, with its sunset provisions and multiple revisions, continue to pose a threat to Constitutionally guaranteed freedoms in the First and Fourth Amendments. It remains to be seen whether the liberties ceded in the name of "increased safety and security" can be reclaimed by *We, the People,* at a future date. History and the oddsmakers would seem to be against such a reversal. Power is an intoxicant like no other, and once obtained, it drives those who wield it to great lengths to retain and increase it. With election integrity a giant question mark in the contemporary American polity model, anything short of revolution or death would seem impotent for dislodging power from those intent on keeping it.

The Best of Intentions

AMERICA WAS CAUGHT napping on September 11, 2001. Given the nature of the terrorist attacks that day and the implication of foreign actors, clearly, additional security measures were needed to protect U.S. citizens and national interests. The original Patriot Act was intended to provide such safeguards. Not unlike mushrooms silently and secretly sprouting from the forest floor, the legislation gave rise to a sharp increase in Federal powers and the establishment of new agencies like The Department of Homeland Security. In retrospect—given the increasingly partisan nature of social discourse since the early 2000s—it was just a matter of time until "reasonable security measures" were turned inward to the detriment of American citizens and the Constitution itself.

This is not the American Dream. Nor is it in alignment with the Founder's thoughts on Natural Law and the preservation of God-given Liberty by the ruling authorities and in accordance with the "consent of the governed." For some 250 years America has employed the democratic process to craft a Republic wherein the rights of the people are arbitrated and legislated by those whom they sent as representatives in various elected offices. The lubricant in the machinery of common interests of a republic is moral integrity—that of the people *and* their representatives. Absent this lubricant the machine will eventually seize up.

This renders Leo Strauss's statement on the matter all the more pressing in our day:

> *"Does this nation in its maturity still cherish the faith in which it was conceived and raised? Does it still hold those 'truths to be self-evident'?"*[8]

Strauss alludes to the "truths" found in the Declaration of Independence and later undergirded by the U.S. Constitution. But these truths—though self-evident—are no longer taught to the very citizens who most need to understand them. Instead, our culture, media, politicians, and pundits advocate the primacy of identity, self-interest, and equity. In a brilliantly destructive strategy, activist educators, legislators, jurists, and influencers have captured the hearts and minds of impressionable young Americans and set them to work destroying the fabric of our nation based on insufficient knowledge of American history, civics, and politics.

All of which lends a haunting quality to Benjamin Franklin's response to Elizabeth Willing Powel's question at the conclusion of the Constitutional Convention of 1787:

> *"Well, Doctor (Franklin), what have we got, a republic or a monarchy?"*

> *"A republic, if you can keep it."*[9]

Earlier, Franklin, then 81 years old, had addressed President George Washington and those in the assembly in Philadelphia in part with these words:

> *"I confess that there are several parts of this Constitution which I do not at present approve, but I am not sure I shall never approve them. For having lived long, I have experienced many instances of being obliged by better information, or fuller consideration, to change opinions even on important subjects, which I once thought right, but found to be otherwise. It is therefore that, the older I grow, the more apt I am to doubt my own judgment, and to pay more respect to the judgment of others."*

> *"In these sentiments, Sir, I agree to this Constitution, with all its faults, if they are such; because I think a General Government necessary for us, and there is no form of government, but what may be a blessing to the peo-*

ple if well administered; and believe further, that this is likely to be well administered for a course of years, and can only end in despotism, as other forms have done before it, when the people shall become so corrupted as to need despotic government."

The question before us as 2023 draws to a close is this: Have *We, the People,* become so corrupted as to need a "despotic government?" If that is the case, can this despotic government succeed as "leader of the free world" once her enemies—and allies—discern her moral decay? Will not her enemies at some point seize the opportunity afforded by the resultant internal chaos and seek to take her place on the world stage?

Lastly, this thought from the bible:

"Pride goes before destruction, And a haughty spirit before a fall." —Proverbs 16:18

Despite her present wretched fiscal, ethical, and moral condition, America remains unabashedly proud. Pride in the most tenuous of propositions has captured our nation's attention with haughty eyes fixed on the latest shiny object, unaware of the dangers of mass narcissistic myopia. There are no blinders quite as effective as pride and arrogance.

PART-VII | AMERICA, THE BEAUTIFUL

Born in a Bubble

THE DAYS OF MY YOUTH were a glorious tapestry of endless playtime and happy family memories. In the early 1960s children could safely play outdoors and news of atrocities like kidnapping, murder, war, and riots was rare. It's not that bad things did not happen. In fact, they were happening all around the globe at that time, for such is the plight of humanity. But in our little hamlet, tucked away in the far northwest corner of Orange County, California, the sun was shining on us continually. Literally and figuratively.

Schoolyards were open and accessible, and my boisterous tribe of late Baby Boomers roamed the fields of nearby *Macy Elementary School* from morning till dark. Our pick up games of football, baseball, and basketball allowed us the freedom to dare and dream as we grew strong and tall. We would play hit-the-bat on the side streets surrounding our neighborhood and often one or two of the dads would join in. When the inevitable car came down the road, we'd scatter to the curbs until the coast was clear. And then the game would resume until my father's special whistle would call us to the dinner table.

When mom had the goods ready to serve, dad would amble out to the corner, tweet out his specific "come home now" cadence—audible for miles we thought—and we would dutifully bid our friends farewell until the morrow when our endless fun-and-games would pick up right where they left off. Truly, this period of my youth was the sweet spot of our age, the intersection of well-being, peace, and prosperity in the wide and deep American middle class of the 1960s. Truly, America, the Beautiful.

Gathering Storm Clouds

I WAS SOON TO LEARN in graphic detail that the glorious bubble between the end of World War II and spiraling hostilities in Southeast Asia was losing air fast. The first and most jarring memory of social upheaval in my lexicon was the assassination of President John F. Kennedy in November, 1963.[10] At that time there were just three television networks and no cable or satellite channels at all. I remember watching the horse-drawn wagon slowly carrying the president's flag-draped casket through the streets of Washington, D.C., in glorious black-and-white. Unfortunately, the President's assassination—captured "live" on the Zapruder film—was shown in color.[11]

The television networks ABC, NBC, and CBS, all carried the same video feed. This ensured that the entirety of America—at least those with television sets at the time—witnessed what is commonly referred to as "The end of Camelot."[12] As if this was not the most shocking thing witnessed by Americans en masse, the assassinations of Robert Kennedy *(the President's brother)* and civil rights leader, Dr. Martin Luther King, in April and June of 1968 slammed the door on the notion that the America we had known until then would ever be the same.

And, it was not.

Coming Full Circle

IN THE MIDDLE OF THE whirlwind of the late 1960s, my brother enlisted in the U.S. Army, and departed to fulfill his patriotic duty in the Vietnam War. At this point in my life, with more days behind me than ahead of me, I am very glad that my brother returned whole from that wretched "conflict." Many did not. Had our family been robbed of its first-born son, I'm not sure I would have been able to recover and put the event into proper perspective for a very long time. If ever.

I have gotten to know Roger better in our latter years. We began attending *La Habra High School* football games together around 2002 when the team emerged from decades of anonymity and began the golden era that saw the *Highlanders* collect seven CIF Southern Section Division Championships over the ensuing 20 seasons.[13] The games presented an easy time to chat and reminisce. Or simply to watch the action on the field, a shared experience that all brothers should be able to enjoy together. I am grateful that we were afforded that time.

Allegiance to Whom?

THE INSTITUTION OF human government is God's idea. God commands Christians to respect and obey the governmental authorities placed over them with few caveats—one being that those in authority cannot compel their subjects to disobey God. Some 3,600 years ago in Egypt, fearing a future uprising from the expanding Hebrew population in Goshen, Pharaoh commanded the Hebrew midwives to kill all male Hebrew babies at birth. Hence, the midwives faced a moral dilemma: Obey man or obey God?

Their choice was difficult but straightforward. The midwives chose not to obey Pharoah—the governmental authority over their lives. Pharaoh called them on the carpet for an explanation, which they provided.[14] But, their true motivation was this: They feared God. As a result, God favored the midwives and "provided households for them." And the Hebrew nation *"multiplied and grew very mighty."*

In a perfect world, everyone would acknowledge, love, and obey God. And all would be well on this planet. However, lasting peace on earth is for a time yet to come. Until then, God has left us with lasting impressions of His Sovereignty extended through governmental authorities who—when they uphold righteousness and punish evil—are very worthy of their calling. In God's plan, rulers must be the benefactors of their subjects:

> *Let every soul be subject to the governing authorities.* ***For there is no authority except from God, and the authorities that exist are appointed by God.*** *Therefore whoever resists the authority resists the ordinance of God, and those who resist will bring judgment on themselves.* ***For rulers are not a terror to good works, but to evil.*** *Do you want to be unafraid of authority? Do what is good, and you will have praise from the same. For he is God's minister to you for good. But if you do evil, be afraid; for he does not bear the sword in vain;* ***for he is God's minister, an avenger to execute wrath on***

him who practices evil. Therefore you must be subject, not only because of wrath but also for conscience's sake.
—Romans 13:1-5

Perspectives

I AM NOT A SOLDIER, nor am I a politician. I am a speck of dust living out a brief existence before meeting my Maker and transitioning into a glorious eternity unfathomable from an earthly perspective. I do not know much, but one thing I do know is that soldiers are the essential citizens of a world in turmoil.

A civilization without soldiers would quickly simmer into a stew of warring tribes and violent self-interests. By comparison, politicians appear to be the chief purveyors of social unrest and political madness in their quest for power. History has shown that politicians cannot long exist without soldiers to stir their pot in distant lands. On the existential recipe card of life, soldiers are an essential ingredient. Politicians appear to be optional.

In America, the Commander-in-Chief of all military forces, the President, is a civilian. Yet he oversees a military of staggering dimensions. America would have suffered many coups since the Revolution without this counterbalance of military and civilian interests. So, the Founders conceived an excellent plan. And yet, a commander-in-chief who contemplates military engagement with a finger to the political wind or with conflicting interests in mind imperils a nation. When this happens, Vietnam—or worse—is the result.

Iraq, Afghanistan, Syria, Somalia. Ukraine. There are seemingly endless violent, dead-end destinations awaiting the arrival of American GIs. And our soldiers are willing to go there—to go anywhere—if they sense a just cause, a righteous endeavor, a holy pursuit. However, the sending powers should never deploy soldiers unless they are intent on victory and are willing to let soldiers be soldiers. The rules of engagement are simple: Find the enemy, engage the enemy, and destroy the enemy. Then, come home.

It is well-said that *"war is hell"*—a true statement. To that end, and with all future military entanglements in mind, I respectfully submit this petition to America's civilian-military leader:

Honorable Commander in Chief—

Do not leverage military conflict for political advantage. Allow your soldiers to attack the enemy with vigor and with fierce finality. Limit the engagement to the irreducible minimum number of days. You'll save countless lives by doing so.

Realize that the only language known to bullies is bullying: A swift blow to the nose followed by boots to the ribs, face, and neck. Therefore, as Commander in Chief, your primary military strategy should be to direct your troops to pummel global bullies into submission or the grave—post haste.

There have always been traitors—those who live in the United States, enjoy its many benefits, yet hate American ideals. These quislings are as treacherous as foreign enemies. Your God-given responsibility is to preserve, protect, and defend the Constitution of the United States from their efforts to destroy it.

Finally, the level of integrity with which you engage your weighty role will determine whether our nation's peace and prosperity wax or wane.

Respectfully,

Ronald G. Kays, Author: Echoes of Vietnam | A Soldier's Voice is Heard

---

[1] The Visual Journalism Team (2021, August 26). *Kabul airport attack: What do we know?* BBC.co.uk. Retrieved November 8, 2023, from https://www.bbc.co.uk/news/world-asia-58349010

[2] Keane, L. (2023, October 10). *Weapons Abandoned by Biden Administration Appear in Hamas Terror Attacks.* Nssf.org. Retrieved October 23, 2023, from https://www.nssf.org/articles/weapons-abandoned-by-biden-administration-appear-in-hamas-terror-attacks/

[3] Seldin, Jeff (2022, April 8). *Pentagon Downplays $7B in US Military Equipment Left in Afghanistan.* VOAnews.com. Retrieved November 8, 2023, from https://www.voanews.com/a/pentagon-downplays-7-billion-in-us-military-equipment-left-in-afghanistan/6549546.html

[4] Wolf, Zachary B. (2023, September 21). *$113 Billion: Where the US investment in Ukraine aid has gone.* CNN.com. Retrieved November 8, 2023, from https://www.cnn.com/2023/09/21/politics/war-funding-ukraine-what-matters/index.html

[5] McDougall, A. J. (2023, April 19). *14 U.S. Special Forces Were in Ukraine Last Month, Leaked Docs Show.* Thedailybeast.com. Retrieved October 23, 2023, from https://www.thedailybeast.com/14-us-special-forces-were-in-ukraine-in-march-pentagon-leak-shows

[6] Harvard University (circa 2023). *Text of the Declaration of Independence.* declaration.fas.harvard.edu. Retrieved November 8, 2023, from https://declaration.fas.harvard.edu/resources/text

[7] India, McKinney; Crocker, Andrew (April 16, 2020). *Yes, Section 215 Expired: Now What?* Eff.org. Retrieved November 8, 2023, from https://www.eff.org/deeplinks/2020/04/yes-section-215-expired-now-what

[8] Sabo, Mike (April 28, 2017). *The American Founders Knew a Virtuous Republic Requires Virtuous People.* theFederalist.com. Leo Strauss quote retrieved November 8, 2023, from https://thefederalist.com/2017/04/28/the-american-founders-knew-a-virtuous-republic-requires-virtuous-people/

[9] Independence National Historical Park (September 22, 2023). *September 17, 1787: A Republic: If You Can Keep It.* NPS.gov. Retrieved November 8, 2023 from https://www.nps.gov/articles/000/constitutionalconvention-september17.htm

[10] History.com editors (April 25, 2023). *Assassination of John F. Kennedy.* history.com. Retrieved November 9, 2023, from https://www.history.com/topics/us-presidents/jfk-assassination

[11] Wikipedia (Circa 2023) *Zapruder Film.* en.wikipidia.org. Retrieved November 9, 2023, from https://en.wikipedia.org/wiki/Zapruder_film

[12] Stamper, Peta (November 18, 2021). *Inside The Myth: What Was Kennedy's Camelot?* historyhit.com. Retrieved November 9, 2023, from https://www.historyhit.com/inside-the-myth-what-was-kennedys-camelot/

[13] US Sports Camps (Circa 2023) *Coach Profile: Frank Mazzotta.* ussportscamps.com. Retrieved November 9, 2023, from https://www.ussports-camps.com/coaches/frank-mazzotta

[14] Bible Gateway (circa 2023). So the king of Egypt called for the midwives and said to them, "Why have you done this thing, and saved the male children alive?" And the midwives said to Pharaoh, "Because the Hebrew women *are* not like the Egyptian women; for they *are* lively and give birth before the midwives come to them." Therefore God dealt well with the midwives, and the people multiplied and grew very mighty. Exodus 1:18-20, New King James Version. Retrieved November 8, 2023, from https://www.biblegate-way.com/passage/?search=Exodus+1%3A18-20&version=NKJV

About the Author

Ron Kays spent nearly four decades in marketing and content development for a major national insurance company before retiring in 2020.

He and his wife, Vicki, live near the Blue Ridge mountains of North Carolina.

Read more at https://linktr.ee/rgkpublishing.

About the Publisher

RGK Publishing creates spiritually and socially relevant content for everyone.

Discover **RGKP** creative services here: https://linktr.ee/rgkpublishing

Read more at https://rgkpublishing.substack.com/.

www.ingramcontent.com/pod-product-compliance
Lightning Source LLC
Chambersburg PA
CBHW070550160726
48003CB00005B/1988